- Hypno Machines -

How To Convert Every Object In Your Environment As a Device For Psychological and Emotional Manipulations

Jack N. Raven

Jack N. Raven

Hypno Machines - How To Convert Every Object In Your Environment As a Device For Psychological and Emotional Manipulations

No part of this book may be reproduced or transmitted in any form whatsoever, electronic, or mechanical, including photocopying, recording, or by any informational storage or retrieval system without express permission from the author.

Copyright © 2013 Jack N. Raven Publishing Company

All rights reserved.

ISBN-13:
978-1492705499

ISBN-10:
1492705497

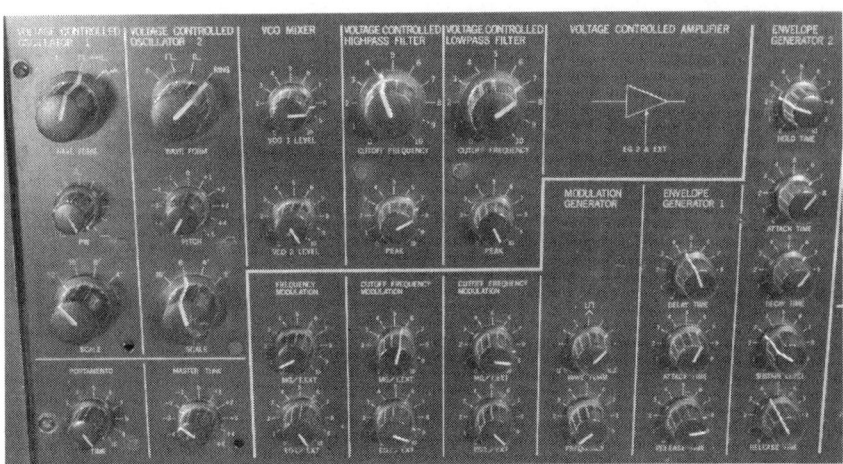

TABLE OF CONTENTS

ABOUT ANCHORS _____ 3
WHAT CAN BE ANCHORED? _____ 3
    EXAMPLES OF ANCHORS _____ 4
INVISIBLE ANCHORS _____ 5
ANCHORS IN MEDIA _____ 6
ANCHORS IN SEDUCTION _____ 6
ANCHORS IN CHANGE WORK _____ 7
THE DIFFERENT KINDS OF ANCHORS _____ 7
STATIC ANCHORS _____ 8
SLIDING ANCHORS _____ 8
MIXING BOWL OF EMOTIONS _____ 10
WHAT MAKES A GOOD ANCHOR _____ 11
    EXAMPLES OF INTENSE STATES THAT NEED DELIBERATE ASSISTANCE _____ 12
ANCHORS WITH SUBLIMINAL EFFECTS _____ 13
THE SPECIFICS _____ 15
RITUAL MAGICK _____ 16
PLAN OF ATTACK _____ 17
SAMPLE CASE STUDY _____ 19
    I LET'S CONDUCT AN ENVIRONMENTAL INVENTORY _____ 19
    II IDENTIFY THE SEPARATE STATES THAT CONTRIBUTE TO THE MAIN STATE ____ 19
        Using the bed _____ 23
MAINTENANCE WORK ON THE TRIGGERS _____ 25
    Other books by Jack N. Raven Publishing _____ 27
    Effortlessly _____ 36

About Anchors

The idea of anchors came from NLP and it means creating memory connections on to triggers that when you activate that trigger, the experience is put back into awareness. You begin seeing what you saw, feeling what you felt and hearing what you heard. It's a way to get back to a past experience.

For practical purposes anchors are used to help you get back in those states perhaps too complicated to manually manufacture each and every time.

People who do anchors treat them as pushbutton mechanisms which allow the operator to flash back into a past experience.

Like normal memory triggers, anchors are not designed to make you remember the facts. Rather they are designed to make you re-experience something you have programmed or made the anchor for.

Some experiences are too intense for them to be contained by anchors alone therefore must be assisted consciously. What it means is when normal experiences are containable by anchors, that's when you fire off the anchor and automatically get the experience.

What can be anchored?

The right question to ask is what cannot be anchored?

Practically anything can be programmed to a button or a trigger just like of you would program a hotkey on a computer to start up a computer process or a program once that hotkey is pressed

This book is all about doing exactly that. You can practically organize your internal and external experiences by making the world into a virtual machine, filled with thousands of buttons and machine levers and knobs.

This is a far better way to organize our experiences and memories by associating them or programming them into anchors that we can manipulate. Whether we do these things deliberately or not we are actually creating anchors of the time and we have been since the beginning.

Examples of anchors

When you were 12 years old think of a song that was catchy at the time. If you were to hear that on the radio at this very moment what would you think of?

If you were to smell that cologne, scent or whatever perfume of your first love that you've broken up with, while walking on the mall what would the experience be?

Wouldn't you instantly flash back into the past see what she saw feel what you felt and just see these flashbacks of memories when you were together with her.?

Invisible anchors

As mentioned we have been creating anchors since the beginning and not necessarily know about it. Some anchors are stronger than others while some are too subtle for us to notice.

Just know that we naturally make associations with our senses and experiences. Whether we are conscious of the process are not we do this all the time. Know these associations and realize that some are beneficial while some ruin us.

An example of a negative anchor is how we associate smoking and socializing. When we are at work the only time to smoke is during lunch breaks and smoke breaks. After sometime and enough number of repetitions, we begin associating cigarettes to chatting up friends, rest and relaxation from work.

Another negative example is during childhood when a child has one of his tantrums the unsuspecting mom gives more attention and love to the kid trying to calm him down. Not knowing that she is actually rewarding bad behavior and has anchored the tantrum with the mother's affection and attention. The child is going to be seeking this behavior in the future and you can bet that is not the end of it.

Anchors in media

If you wondered about these fashion and perfume commercials with abstract pictures and images that don't really make sense intellectually? This is a form of anchoring where they connect or associate the over all experience and insinuations and subtexts with the brand.

The more repetitions and the more exposure to different forms of media to the audience, eventually the perfume brand name becomes synonymous with the concept or idea that is being anchored by the advertising campaign. Abstract ideas can be anchored or associated with a brand name. The mere mention or seeing the brand evokes these ideas in the audience's head.

Company logos are also an example of anchoring abstract concepts to symbolic figures that do nothing but represent specific ideas they connect to the brand logo.

Anchors in seduction

You may use this technology in seduction and perhaps the objective is to create amazing feelings and experiences and for all those ideas to be frozen and associated with your voice, face and your over all essence.

This can actually get sneakier, manipulative and more pervasive than that. Deliberate anchor installations and manipulations are employed by NLP styled seduction artist. Read through the book and you will gather enough to create your own regimen for this purpose.

Anchors in change work

Basically is about anchoring helpful or useful resource states that you'd like to keep and be able to use over and over automatically. In some ways it's like pressing the remote and it triggers the states and feelings instantly.

The same goes for negative states where they are anchored to be either eliminated completely or at least kept in check or minimized. States such as depression, sadness, anger can also be anchored and then manipulated accordingly depending on the intentions of the operator.

The different kinds of anchors

As said previously anything can be converted to an anchor. Any idea, sound, taste, smell any idea at all can be turned to anchors.

You can even stack anchors, mix and match them together to create new ones. Perhaps a new invention that does not exist anywhere else.

Again using the metaphor of button pushing of machines, where you mix and match and greatly expand this by pushing the right mixture of buttons. Or you can think of it as cooking and there are special recipes where you can make designer states for yourself. Such is the power anchors.

Static anchors

This is the most common kind of anchor where you think of the state and try to get an intense state and you can associate that by pressing on a body part. Do enough repetitions and the anchor gets alive. This is an on off button. You press on the switch and you receive a jolt of that state. It's not permanent of course, so you have to repeatedly push or trigger the button.

Sliding anchors

These are very much like static anchors except you're using a different metaphor of a volume knob or any machine equalizer lever of some sort.

These are more powerful because these are not crude on and off switches. You can actually increase the intensity or volume of any of the states.

Programming the anchor is similar to creating static anchors where you associate the state to a body part except this button is an analog button where you can adjust the volume.

In order to program this, find a state or experience and when you are about to reach near the peak of the experience, press a body part or whatever you want to create an anchor for. Do enough repetitions until you have successfully created the sliding anchors.

Once the static, on/off switch anchor has been created (incidentally the same process for the static anchor above) you can then go into next step which is calibrating or programming it to be an analog switch.

For this example let's say you want to program the state of happiness. By pressing on your forefingers you start getting that state of happiness. Keep it for about two seconds pressing the forefingers and then break state by thinking of something else completely nonsense such as adding 5+5 or think of baby powder etc. whatever it is does not matter.

Now that you done this enough times and when you press on the fore fingers you automatically get the state of happiness. The next step is to turn it into a volume knob or slider. You can do this by however which way you want, but for this example let's say that when you place your forefingers to the right, it intensifies the feeling of happiness. When you twist to the left it weakens it to zero. Just keep on practicing and programming it from zero to full volume until you are convinced that the anchor has been set correctly.

Do that with a body part, any object anything at all!

Another variation of the sliding anchor is let's say a lighter. Hold the lighter in front of you. That becomes the neutral state. When you push out the lighter farther, the state weakens. The closer it gets the more intense it becomes.

Do the same process as above repeatedly calibrating and programming the anchors to respond and work as we designed.

Any thing that can involve movement can be turned to a sliding anchor.

You can use ball pens and the more you encircle on the paper the stronger it becomes. Insert go to the left spinning counterclockwise it weakens the state and vice versa.

Mixing bowl of emotions

I said previously you can anchor on anything and any idea or feeling, any concept at all.

Let's say you have 10 marbles and each marble can be programmed as a static anchor for different states. You can program one marble as happiness, the next funny, the next passion for life so on. You can then mix them up in a bowl and as you do, you also get the feeling of combining different states together. You have to make this happen, willing it to happen.

With that example we used physical objects which are the marbles. However they don't have to be physical at all and can be imaginary objects. Do the same example with the marbles except they're just imaginary. The bowl itself can even be imaginary.

On top of that you can make physical objects anchor to an imaginary one. So choose a perfume and program the scent to mean lust. It's the same process as programming a static anchor that when you smell it you'd think of the state of lust. Hold it for a few seconds, break state, think of nonsense, and go at it again do it repeatedly a few times until the anchor is set correctly.

Once the perfume anchor has been set, you can then mix it with the imaginary marbles and see the experience of creating new states.

Literally anything and everything can be converted to an anchor and you can manipulate them accordingly depending on what purpose they serve for you.

What makes a good anchor

You must be anchoring near the peak of any state. As with the happiness state example, when you anchor the state when it isn't even clear to you or that you're not really seeing or feeling happiness at that moment, the weak state is what gets programmed.

Because anchors are never as intense as original states, so you have to factor that in when you program. Some states are too intense for them to work automatically so they need to be assisted deliberately by the conscious mind.

However you can maximize the effects of anchoring by seeking to always reaching the peak or maximum state and repeatedly programming and reprogramming as many times as necessary, in different times not just in one sitting.

Examples of intense states that need deliberate assistance

Have you ever been in a high energy party or a concert where you are shouting at the top of your lungs, extremely high energy fun and yet exhausting?

This is the kind of state that you can't just program automatically because it requires a lot of energy and emotional effort on your part. We're trying to anchor that intensity and indeed you can imagine being in that state. But are you really?

Imagine you are shouting really loud, partying crazy but it's not exactly the same as actually being there feeling the same height our with explosive intensity.

If you intend on anchoring these intense states, I would highly suggest you create steppingstone states to help you pump you up until you reach those high level states.

So you have to stair step your way up and when you

reach that state? It's easier to return because now you have a combination of stair step anchors to predictably and reliably get you to those hard to get intense highly charged high-energy high-octane states of mind and physicality. When firing off the anchor goes through the same process and sequence until you can get back to that state consistently.

Anchors with subliminal effects

We could program anchors with the desire for it to have observable state changes. But the effects are far-reaching that in addition to the observable state changes, they also are able to program effects on the subliminal level.

By subliminal, it means below conscious awareness which nonetheless work anyway. We may not experience the effect overtly, but rest assured the effects are happening invisibly below conscious awareness.

This is important to note before we get to the next portion where we are going to be reprogramming literally everything available to us in the environment, to help us affect the changes we want.

Depending on the time and effort you can put in to this work the effects that are a bit weak which require deliberate conscious mind assistance will still work but only subliminally , as said previously. The programmings will still work, but may take longer to work.

Imagine if in your house there are 1000 objects and each one is actually a trigger doing invisible work that helps you get closer to your goals? Practically everything there has been converted to a Psychological machine that does the work invisibly and automatically. The possibilities are endless!

Another benefit is if you have not made the connection yet is that although we are talking in the context of doing the work for us personally? The same technology can be exploited as a persuasion tool to affect others. If you can control the environment and convert everything as an anchor to create the effects you wanted on the target, they will work automatically.

If you ever been in the long relationship and when you break up everything just seems to remind you of that person or the activities you've done with that person. That is how anchoring the environment works!

Practically everything in the world is a sending out a message broadcasting the memory you shared with this person. Some individuals actually have to move out of the house just to kill the old memories or anchors bothering them, which have been automatically and invisibly set by people who haven't have the faintest notion of what an anchor is.

They work whether you want to or not. Whether you know them or not. The effectiveness is just a matter of programming them correctly through proper repetition and intensity.

The specifics

Now that you are aware of the different kinds of anchors, let us explore the benefits and how can we use it to improve our lives.

Everything, literally everything that we do in life can be converted to an anchor and since we have established that anchors can control states and any concept existing in our minds, it means that we can take more control of our states by just naturally operating in the world paying attention to this power.

We can turn our bodies and fill it with pushbutton mechanisms that directly affect our feelings and states.

We can convert the doorknobs, light switches, hitting the keyboard, moving the mouse, twisting the steering wheel, starting the ignition of the car, programming every step we take to affect any state we desire to manipulate, how we drink, how we eat etc,EVERYTHING!

Not only we can reprogram the images we see in the world to become anchors. For example the sunlight shining on our face, the wind blowing our hair, the sound waves reverberating our bodies etc. can all be exploited.

Instead of letting them go to waste, ignoring the why

not convert them to automatic state changers, that work automatically whether we put deliberate effort on them or not.

Not only can states be affected, but any concept as well!

If you practice any sort of energy work like magick, Witchcraft, Qigong, etc, everything can be exploited for this purpose as well. The objective being to manipulate energies- psychic energies instead of our states and emotions.

Anything you can imagine, feel, taste, smell, touch, experience can be preserved and be manipulated mechanically through the use of these anchors.

Ritual Magick

Before we proceed let us talk about Ritual or ceremonial magick. This has ideas and similarities that as you'll soon see are also applicable with the work we'll about to do.

The most famous ceremonial magick we do, without even really understanding its roots and history are weddings!

Ceremonial magick is about conducting a magickal ritual where the actions and gestures represent ideas and powers, including the objects and the special words and gestures uttered in the ceremony.

Instead of imaginary, mental concepts and pure mental

imagery, these ideas are replaced and physicalized by actual, tangible and observable actions and objects.

Imagination feels more real, tangible if it is converted to something physical!

Everything there, the ring, the procession, the veil, the kiss etc, are symbolic of ideas! They are really just "Symbolic Morphology" which we shall talk about in a few moments.

Plan of attack

What we are trying to do here, is literally commandeer anything and everything in the universe to be exploited for our purpose in terms of change work. It may take a bit of initial effort to program everything up, but once set? There's almost no work involved anymore except if we need to deliberately assist some of the anchors or do maintenance re-anchoring. Some anchor dies down a little each day that passes, therefore must be recharged.

A good visual to explain this is that were making external and physical connections (see them as electronic wires) to the invisible and abstract, mental ideas and feelings so that we are able to manipulate them as if we are pushing on the remote.

 The effects are far reaching and are actually dependent on exactly what you want to achieve, and the level of competence and know how on what you know about change work. Meaning if you know any other techniques, you can supplement it by having this mindset of having deliberate control of the invisible of anchoring everything.

You can even modify and use the concepts presented here to work with other visualizations and meditation systems you may be currently doing regardless of which system that is. Our main objective is to <u>convert these ideas to physical things that we can touch and manipulate</u>. Not only does it make it real for us but the effects are stronger when treated in this fashion.

Imagining a ball of light is not as strong as actually seeing the blinding ball of light which is the sun.

So whatever visualizations and mental imagery you may be doing for whatever work the effects are magnified whenever you physicalize and convert them to anchors.

Some of the effects will work on the feelings level. Some work on the emotional or changing of state levels. Some only work invisibly, in terms of effect that they only work on a subliminal level. Others become as memory pegs that just remind you on a logical level about the concept without affecting your states.

Play around with these tools and you'll begin to see how to play with these in ways you've never thought of.

Sample case study

Although we can create many anchors for different purposes, for this case study will going to focus on one objective which would consist of many different states of to achieve the results we want.

Let's say our goal is to develop our persuasion skills.

What are the existing things we can exploit for this purpose? For this example we're going to minimize the size of the environment this to a small studio apartment and let's assume that you are only anchoring what is inside this apartment. But obviously you're not stuck to just that and we can exercise the same principles and concepts outside the apartment when you are going to do this for real.

I Let's conduct an environmental inventory

Inside the studio apartment is a plasma television, computer, air-conditioning, a fan, remote control, a refrigerator, light switches, lighting, a bed, a coach, a treadmill, water faucet and a bathtub.

So now we're going to be converting all these devices inside the apartment into our devices of state change.

II Identify the separate states that contribute to the main state

For the topic of Persuasion skills, there are many factors but for this example we'll shorten it three items.

a. Deep empathy

b. Killer instinct to go for the close

c. Ability to make the offer extremely beautiful and valuable, that has to be bought NOW!

For the three elements we can program each item with one quality or have all the qualities programmed to each item. However it could be difficult to imagine so you probably wouldn't do it that way and instead have a 1:1 ratio with quality to every object in the house.

The studio apartment itself, just being inside there can be programmed with the one major onset i.e. persuasion powers, or as said previously the separate smaller states that make up the main state.

In order to do this you have to will that whenever you're inside the location, it automatically and naturally programs you on the many different components of persuasion. The way to phrase it is that each and every moment you spend inside the apartment, effects are working on the many different layers and elements of persuasion and they are working automatically doubling in power more and more as time goes on.

So we are outside the apartment and we command it like this. When we step inside, we'll instantly be filled up or get "cooked" automatically by the powers, regardless if you are aware of the process or not. It's all happening automatically without your permission!

So we break state once again as stated earlier and step out of the room. Once outside notice the feeling of the lack of persuasion rays or energies shining over you, cooking us earlier.

So again we step in and instantly we feel every part of our being is being cooked, increasing our hours in persuasion.

We do that for every room in the house such as the bathroom and the rooms. Because the whole apartment this program for the general idea of persuasive power, so the concept for the bathroom has to be a little bit different and yet under the umbrella of general persuasive power.

So we could probably choose C, which is the ability to make anything sound extremely amazing and beautiful. So do the same process earlier step in and out, in and out a dozen times and instead of general persuasive power we are programming C and the general persuasive power.

Do note that the more we anchor everything we are going to be working on, the more powerful the effects are going to be.

When you visualize something you really have to feel it! Feeling is extremely important with this type of work. You don't just symbolically or visually see your mind becoming more effective in persuasion, but you can actually <u>feel it</u> intensifying however which way you can imagine it.

Perhaps you can imagine that as a pneumatic tire increasing pressure, building up pressure on the inside increasing your power etc.

What about the light switches and the light inside the apartment? You can program that for the killer instinct. Again we'll do the step. When you press it to fuel the state, break state, turning off then turn it on again and you get to feel the state again. When you turn on the lights you can represent it as a metaphor like a light bulb moment as it were to help you imagine even better.

Now we are going to be working with the analog switches in the apartment. The volume knobs and other electronic triggers like the dimmer that are not simple on and off switches.

What are the analog triggers we can use in the house? The doorknobs, the faucet, etc.

Referring back to the sliding anchor earlier, what is more important is calibrating that anchor that when you move to the right it intensifies it, when you turn to the left or counterclockwise it has the opposite effect. We need to do this several times until it's been program permanently and is now operational.

Using the bed

There are many ways to treat it for anchoring. We can create a metaphor where the feeling of resting on it is the actual energizing element to let's say letter A. that the more you sleep on it you are being recharged and intensifying the empathy powers automatically programming you along the way while you energize.

At this juncture we should be talking about metaphors and symbolic morphology to help us create better anchors. Metaphors are the language of the unconscious.

What you have been doing so far is also mixing standard anchoring techniques with metaphors and symbolic morphologies.

Symbolic morphology refers to representing an abstract concept or feeling in physical terms. Because some ideas are so abstract and difficult to imagine or hold in the mind so we use symbolic representations that we can process easily.

The abstract concept of persuasive power can be represented as a color, with a scent if you wish and the sound and feelings alongside it.

For example we see the idea of persuasion power as a blob of light in our minds. The bigger the make it, the more intense the feeling or power becomes. The fainter or dimmer the light, the weaker the feelings become. These are all done imaginatively but as what we've done earlier, we actually associate it with a physical object which is the physical light in the room.

Now that we have converted the concept is to exist only in the mind is now been converted to the physical world. We can now manipulate it to mean whatever we want it to mean.

Notice the light switch we are working on is the different sort, or not the on-off switch type, at this point we have to work with another resource that is analog which is the water faucet.

The stronger the stream of water, the stronger the feelings and vice versa.

Coming back to the bed example, because we have converted the bed as a representation of "A", or the physical embodiment of the abstract concept of deep empathy, so the longer we are physically exposed to it the more it permeates our bodies and every cell to charge on the desired quality working automatically forevermore.

I think you know where we are going with this.

Maintenance work on the triggers

We can do everything in one session and to some extent most anchors do work automatically without the need for recharging. But what is better is the make the anchors produce real sensations as real as the actual physical objects that we can see and touch and this can be done only through many repetitions spread out within a reasonable span of time.

It should feel like the first thing you feel when you go inside the house is a feeling of increasing persuasive power sensations. That no matter what you are thinking of you can't help feeling like how you would feel air-conditioning once you step in. It has to be that real and tangible. It is automatic and undeniable. You are not always aware of the air-conditioning, but when you put your attention to it, it's just there.

If you find an anchor as not working? The answer is always recharging the anchor! Simple as that. Do it enough times and the programming sticks and you can enjoy stronger effects each time you re-program or re-anchor. If it still doesn't get fixed by just one anchor? Then create a bunch of them! Either all have the same message? Or many different anchors that when combined creates the MAIN state change we are after.

ABOUT THE AUTHOR

Jack N. Raven finished AB Legal Management and MBA-Management. He has studied many areas of applied Psychology and persuasion such as Hypnosis, Neuro-Linguistic Programming (equivalent Practitioner and Master Practitioner training level), Sales, traditional Marketing and Online marketing, Search Engine Optimization, Copywriting, Seduction, systems, Sedona Method ™, Emotional Freedom Techniques™. He has over a decade of experience and training in esoteric systems like Qi-Gong, Bardon Hermetics, Keylontic Sciences, Quantum Touch ™ and other energy healing systems. He has studied various martial arts and miscellaneous self improvement systems and technologies.

His current passion is Digital Arts and Fashion Photography.

Please LIKE and SHARE my page to get automatic, future updates to my books:

http://www.facebook.com/jacknraven

Other books by Jack N. Raven Publishing

The Seduction Force Multiplier series

The Seduction Force Multiplier 1- Bring Out Your FULL Seduction powers through

the Power of Routines, Drills, Scripting and Protocols

This is book #1 and a must read if you are serious in exploring and maximizing your seduction potential. Includes more in depth information on how to construct, internalize and the advantages of Scripting versus Natural game convos.

The Seduction Force Multiplier 2 - Scripts and Routines Book

This is the main routines manual which contains the full lines and routines, that are shortened in this book. More than 700 of them!

Also includes the full audio of the routines you can listen to.

The Seduction Force Multiplier 3- PUA Routines Memory Transplant Package

This is book #3 that includes nearly 2 hours of audio. A one of a kind system that allows you to easily memorize about 700 routines and lines from book #2, in just days!

Imagine the dramatic improvements in your game, if you can internalize hundreds of routines! Routines you wont have a problem summoning. All on muscle memory, reflexive, ready to go, just automatically flows out of your mouth without effort in the field!

The Seduction Force Multiplier 4 - Situational PUA Scripts and Routines

In this book, specific routines or scripts have been made focusing on the most common scenarios facing the PUAs.
These are specific game recipes exactly made covering that particular environment or situation! From opening to mid-game, everything is handed to you.

The Seduction Force Multiplier V - Target Auto Response Package

This book covers over 160 target/set reactions so you wont have to rack your brains coming up with responses, and so you can handle each reaction effectively!

Over 900 lines covering 160 reactions so you won't have to rack your brains coming up with effective responses.
Also includes methods to INTERNALIZE/MEMORIZE the material.

Shielded Heart - How To Stop Yourself From Falling For A Seduction Target

For one reason or another you probably don't want to fall in love for that girl or guy. This book is the only book of its kind dealing with this sensitive subject! This will make you invulnerable to strong feelings, in order for you to not fall for a seduction target.

How To Cheat Proof Your Relationships

A thought provoking book, entirely about the subject of seducing someone in a relationship! Either as the aggressor/Player, or the lover wanting to protect his or her love from being seduced by 3rd party Operators and Seducers.

For Inner game development

Secrets to Hacking Your Brain- Be Your Own Therapist

A book on the best techniques from various self help disciplines like NLP, Hypnosis, EFT etc, on how to remove any feelings, and emotions at will!

Hypno Machines - How To Convert Every Object In Your Environment As a Device For Psychological and Emotional Manipulator

Based on the NLP principle of Anchoring, this book will allow you to convert literally everything that exists in the world, as your change agents, that work automatically in the background creating emotional and psychological developments and changes.

The same concept can be used in persuasion too, if you are inclined.

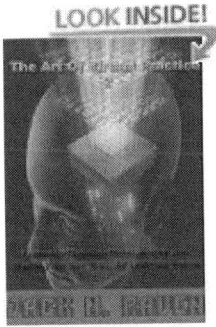

The Art Of Virtual Practice 2 - Learning and Mastery Of Any Skill At Lighting Speeds!

It takes about 10,000 hours to be a MASTER at any craft. By following the techniques on this book? You can cut that that to a fraction of the time!

You can get more field time/practice time by doing these special techniques-anytime, anywhere! Imagine any skill, you can learn to master it at a fraction of the time!

How to Operate with Your Full Potential and Talents

If you've always wanted to perform at your 100% best but couldn't?

Then this is for you!

By figuring out your deepest motivations and "why"s, every part of what you're doing becomes more charged, solid, and FORCEFUL!

You will feel energized, centered, and fully aligned with your full powers, talents and capabilities! Alignment is the key to unlocking your full potential!

How To Master Resilience And Be Invincible To Life's Disappointments And Failures

By developing the proper mindsets, and seeing what these negative, hurtful energies for what they truly are? The reader can strengthen his fortitude, and almost enjoy failures, as a means of reaching the higher levels!

And no, this book won't tell you to live in a fairy tale world, and stay positive all the time!

The X-Factor Manual - Learn How To be A Model Even If You Don't Look Like One

A book for increasing sex appeal, though written with models in mind? The principles and techniques also apply to regular men and women, who want to increase attractiveness using modeling techniques, as well as techniques from other disciplines.

The Age Erase System - Hypnotic Anti Aging Serum

You don't have to settle with getting old. Just with the power of your mind, you can reverse the ravaging effects of time on your health, organs, skin and even looks!

Try this for a month, and tell me it doesn't work! I dare you!

Develop Insane Self Confidence and Naturally Unleash The Supermodel Within

This program will allow you to unleash the hidden gorgeous creature hiding inside of you. This program will easily unleash, in no time at all, your sexy self confidence and sex appeal.
Field tested to give you absolute results!

Persuasion

The Persuaders Guide To Eliminating Resistance And Getting Compliance

If you are a Persuader (who isn't), this book can teach you how to navigate and make your offers to minimize, even eliminate resistance from subjects/targets!

If you can master resistance? You can master persuasion!

Jack N. Raven

The Art of Invisible Compliance - How To Make People Do What You Want Effortlessly

This book includes the Ins and Outs of making people do what you want, as covertly or overtly as you want.
If you've wondered how Intelligence Operatives make people do things short of coercion, this is how they do it.

The principles work in any persuasion setting, whether seduction, sales, marketing, anything that involves getting a desired action(compliance) from people. This book will teach you how to move INVISIBLY to get what you want, without revealing your position yourself! Very useful for covert persuasions.

Goals and Motivation

Unstoppable and Fearless - Know What You Want and Get It

By knowing what you want, you now need the courage to actually get it and win! This book explores and gives you practical steps how you can reduce the fears, and make you unusually comfortable with fears and places outside your comfort zones.

Hypno Machines - How To Convert Every Object In Your Environment As a Device For Psychological and Emotional Manipulations

Just Go- Having The Courage and Will to Pursue Your Dreams

Most people are afraid to go after what they want, let alone actually pursue it! This book will help to set you on your way!

How To Make Better Life Decisions

This book will help you to make crucial life decisions in every facet of life!

It helps give you the tools and elements to consider in weighing the many possible courses of actions and alternatives, to help you choose the absolute best decisions each and every time!

How To Diet Like a Machine- Make Any Diet Program Work With Ease

This book will give you the tools to PERMANENTLY brainwash yourself to loving the new diet meal program. You'll hate it in the beginning, but you'll grow to love it!
Because everyone hates diets, and the only way a sane person will want to keep it, is if gets reprogrammed forcefully!

Made in the USA
Columbia, SC
13 July 2021